PRINT
HANDWRITING
PRACTICE
FOR WRITING FLUENCY

THE SEVEN WONDERS
OF THE ANCIENT WORLD

This Book Belongs To:

_____

_____

SAGUARO BLOOM

ACADEMICS

Print Handwriting Practice for Writing Fluency: The Seven Wonders of the Ancient World: Copywork and Writing Prompts Workbook

How to Use This Book

This book is separated into two sections.

The first section contains information on the seven wonders of the ancient world for writers to trace and copy. Students have the flexibility to write one sentence, one page, or even focus on one wonder at a time.

On the following pages,

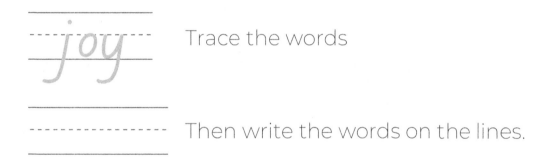

Trace the words

Then write the words on the lines.

The second section is dedicated to writing prompts and activities aimed at fostering students' handwriting fluency and elevating their critical thinking skills. Within this section, you'll find two unique writing prompts for each of the seven wonders. Students may complete one, both, or even none of the prompts for each wonder. These prompts span a spectrum of difficulty levels and encompass diverse writing styles, making them suitable for students with a wide range of skills and interests. Please feel free to adapt and make use of these pages in a manner that best suits your needs.

A a   B b   C c

D d   E e   F f   G g

H h   I i   J j   K k

L l   M m   N n   O o

P p   Q q   R r   S s

T t   U u   V v   W w

X x   Y y   Z z

A a   B b   C c   D d   E e

F f   G g   H h   I i   J j

K k   L l   M m   N n   O o

P p   Q q   R r   S s   T t

U u   V v   W w   X x   Y y

Z z

The Seven Wonders of the Ancient World

Great Pyramid of Giza

Statue of Zeus at Olympia

Temple of Artemis at Ephesus

Mausoleum at Halicarnassus

Colossus of Rhodes

Lighthouse of Alexandria

Hanging Gardens of Babylon

Writing Practice

NAME _____

Philo of Byzantium

Philo of Byzantium created the original list

of the ancient wonders of the world.

He wrote about these wonders in his work

entitled On the Seven Wonders in 225 B.C..

NAME _____

Map of Mediterranean Region

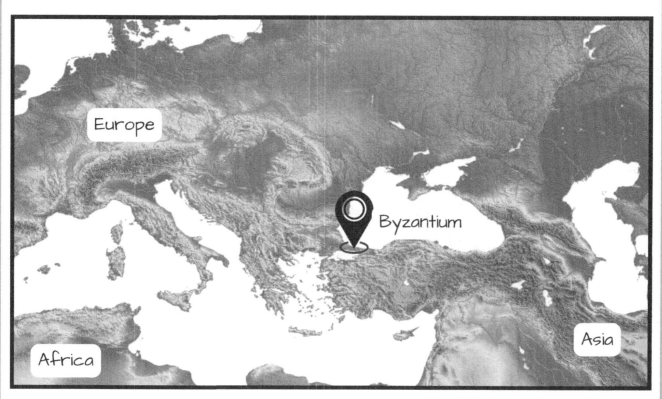

Europe

Byzantium

Africa

Asia

Byzantium is now the modern day city of Istanbul.

Byzantium was a city in Ancient Greece.

NAME _____

Great Pyramid of Giza

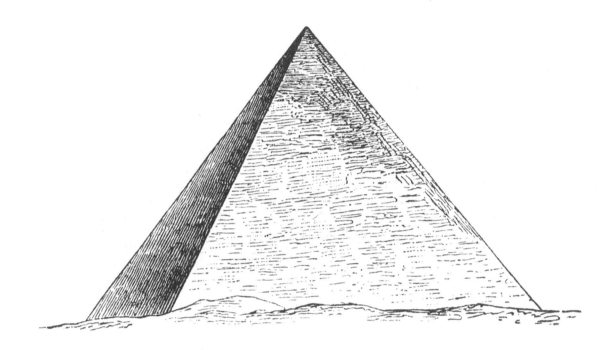

The Great Pyramid, also known as the

Pyramid of Khufu, is one of the most

famous structures in the world.

NAME _____

Great Pyramid of Giza
Map

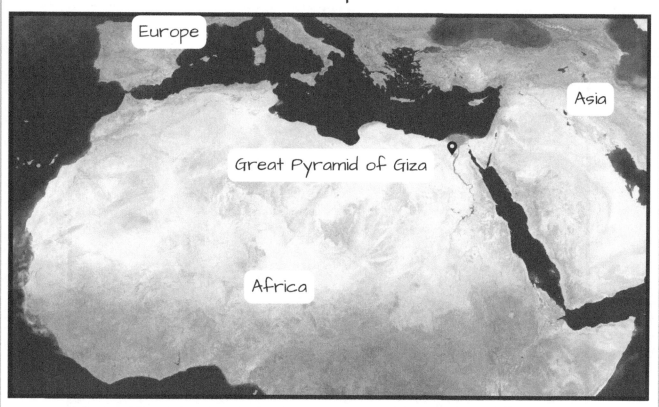

Europe

Asia

Great Pyramid of Giza

Africa

It is located near the city of Giza in Egypt,

along the Nile River. It is the only

ancient wonder still standing.

NAME _____

Great Pyramid of Giza

The Great Pyramid is part of a group of three

pyramids- Khufu, Khafra, and Menkaura.

NAME _____

Great Pyramid of Giza

The Great Pyramid is the oldest

and tallest of these pyramids,

originally standing at 481 feet.

In fact it was taller than any other man- made

structure for almost 4,000 years.

Great Pyramid of Giza

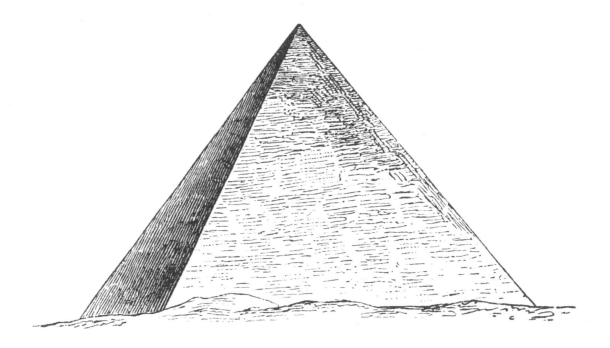

The Great Pyramid was built sometime around

2700 B.C. and 2500 B.C.

NAME _____

Great Pyramid of Giza

It took about 27 years to complete

construction on the pyramid.

The pyramids were built as tombs for

Egyptian pharaohs.

Great Pyramid of Giza

The sphinx was built near the Great

Pyramid of Giza.

NAME _____

Statue of Zeus at Olympia

The Statue of Zeus was a sculpture,

created by the famous Athenian

sculptor Phideas.

The statue was finished sometime around

435 B.C. and then placed in the

temple of Zeus in the city of Olympia.

Statue of Zeus at Olympia

The statue was decorated with gold,

ebony, ivory, and precious stones.

Statue of Zeus at Olympia

This wonder was 40 feet tall and barely

fit in the temple.

The statue showed Zeus sitting on a throne

and carved sphinxes on each armrest.

NAME _____

Statue of Zeus at Olympia
Map

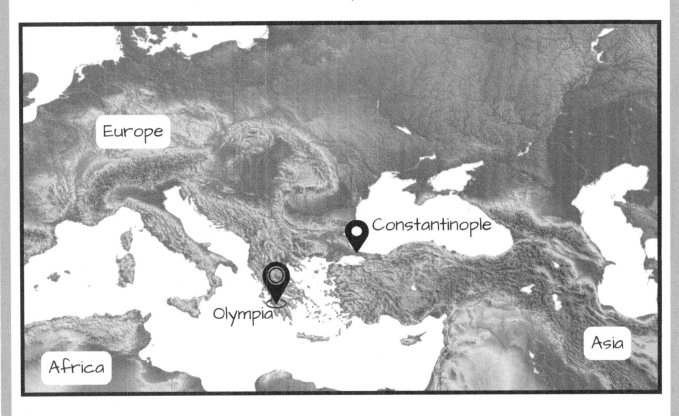

Europe

Constantinople

Olympia

Africa

Asia

It was so impressive it drew visitors from

across the Mediterranean.

NAME _____

Statue of Zeus at Olympia

The statue was later destroyed

but the circumstances of it's

destruction is unknown.

One idea is that the statue was moved

to Constantinople where it was destroyed in

a fire in 475 A.D.

Statue of Zeus at Olympia

The Greeks believed Zeus was the king of the

gods who ruled the sky and thunder.

The Temple of Artemis

The Temple of Artemis was an Ancient

Greek temple built for the goddess Artemis.

It was built in the ancient city of

Ephesus which is in modern day Turkey

by king Croesus of Lydia.

The Temple of Artemis

Croesus funded the building of this temple

after conquering the city around 550 B.C.

The Temple of Artemis

The temple of Artemis was designed

to be a grand marvel showcasing it's

architectural and artistic excellence.

The building was about twice the size of

other Greek buildings.

The Temple of Artemis

Artemis was the Greek goddess of the hunt.

127 columns were decorated with intricate

carvings and statues.

NAME _____

The Temple of Artemis

People came from all over to worship

and leave offerings for Artemis.

Inside the temple, there was a statue of Artemis

made of gold and ivory, crafted by the renowned

Greek sculptor Phidias.

NAME _____

The Temple of Artemis Map

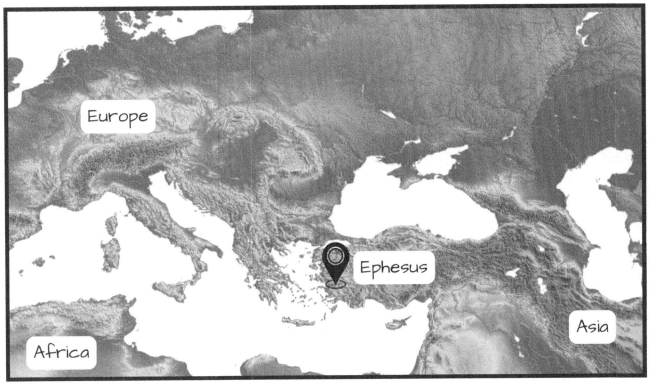

The temple was destroyed and rebuilt

many times, first by arson, earthquakes,

and fighting.

The Temple of Artemis

In 262 A.D. the temple was destroyed by

Ostrogoths and when rebuilt, never regained its

it's former splendor.

The temple met its ultimate demise

when it was destroyed by Christians in 401 A.D.

NAME _____

Mausoleum at Halicarnassus

The Mausoleum at Halicarnassus was

an architectural marvel located in the ancient

city of Halicarnassus (now in modern- day Turkey).

NAME _____

Mausoleum at Halicarnassus

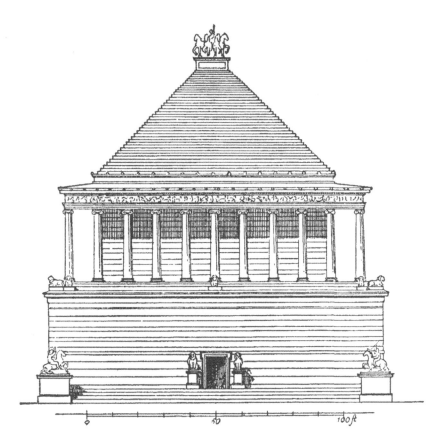

The mausoleum was a tomb built in 353 B.C.

by Mausolus, king of Carnia, and

his wife, Artemesia.

NAME _____

Mausoleum at Halicarnassus

The building was complicated.

It was constructed in three layers.

The first layer was a 60 foot base with steps.

The middle layer was filled with 36 columns

and statues.

NAME _____

Mausoleum at Halicarnassus

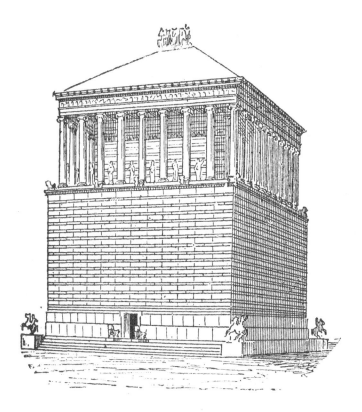

The roof was was pyramid shaped and

a marble chariot with horses rested on top.

NAME _____

Mausoleum at Halicarnassus

In addition to the marble statues and columns,

there were images and scenes carved into

the mausoleum.

The best artists and craftsmen were hired

to decorate the building.

NAME _____

Mausoleum at Halicarnassus
Map

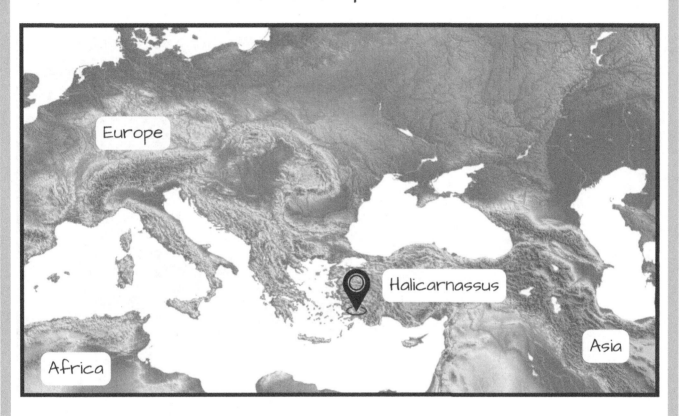

Europe

Halicarnassus

Asia

Africa

The mausoleum was destroyed in the 13th century

from a series of earthquakes.

Colossus of Rhodes
Map

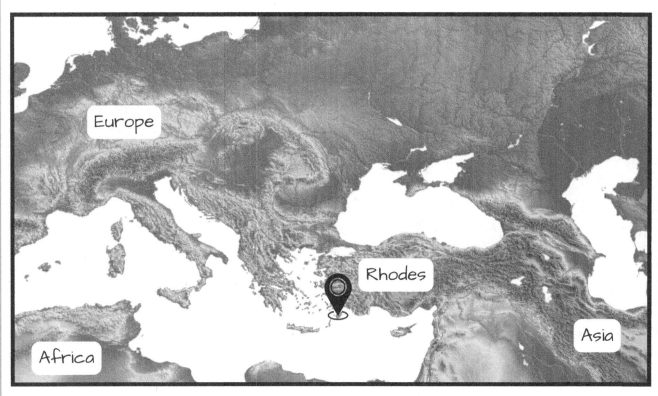

Europe

Rhodes

Asia

Africa

The Colossus of Rhodes was a giant

sculpture that stood on the island of

Rhodes in ancient Greece.

NAME _____

Colossus of Rhodes

The Rhodians hired Chares of Lyndos

to build the bronze statue of the

Greek sun god Helios. It took twelve years

to build and was finished around 280 B.C.

Colossus of Rhodes

Helios

The statue was the tallest statue in the

ancient world, standing at 108 feet tall.

NAME _____

Colossus of Rhodes

The Colossus of Rhodes was reportedly

constructed to commemorate the city

of Rhodes' victorious defense against

an attack by the Macedonians.

Colossus of Rhodes

In 226 B.C., the statue collapsed during

a powerful earthquake.

NAME _____

Colossus of Rhodes

Colossus was never rebuilt and so lay in ruins

until 653 A.D. when the Arabs invaded Rhodes.

It is believed that they may have taken

the bronze metal and sold as scrap.

NAME _____

Lighthouse of Alexandria

The Lighthouse of Alexandria, also called

the Pharos of Alexandria, was another

architectural marvel from ancient Egypt.

NAME _____

Lighthouse of Alexandria

The lighthouse was built on the island of

Pharos to help ships navigate safely into

Alexandria's harbor.

Lighthouse of Alexandria

At night a fired burned at the top

but during the day, mirrors helped guide

ships into port.

NAME _____

Lighthouse of Alexandria

It was one of the tallest structures

of the ancient world, standing at 330 feet tall.

NAME _____

Lighthouse of Alexandria

A series of earthquakes from 953 to

1323 B.C. damaged the lighthouse,

eventually leading to it being abandoned.

However, it was the third- longest surviving

wonder of the world.

NAME _____

Lighthouse of Alexandria
Map

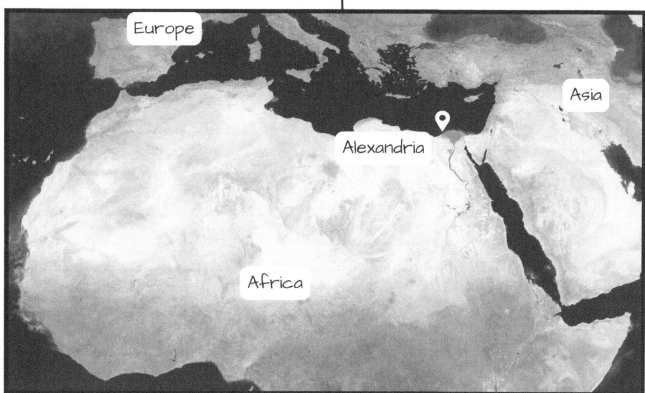

Europe

Asia

Alexandria

Africa

Centuries later, remains of the lighthouse

were found on the bottom of the sea.

Hanging Gardens of Babylon

The Hanging Gardens of Babylon are

an amazing feat of engineering.

Babylonian king Nebuchadnezzar II is often

given credit for building the gardens

as a gift to his wife Amytis.

NAME _____

Hanging Gardens of Babylon

Amytis reportedly missed the green

landscape of her home in Media.

Hanging Gardens of Babylon

The garden was built with a terraced

construction that would have required

a sophisticated irrigation system.

Hanging Gardens of Babylon

Exotic trees and other plants

were on each level.

NAME _____

Hanging Gardens of Babylon
Map

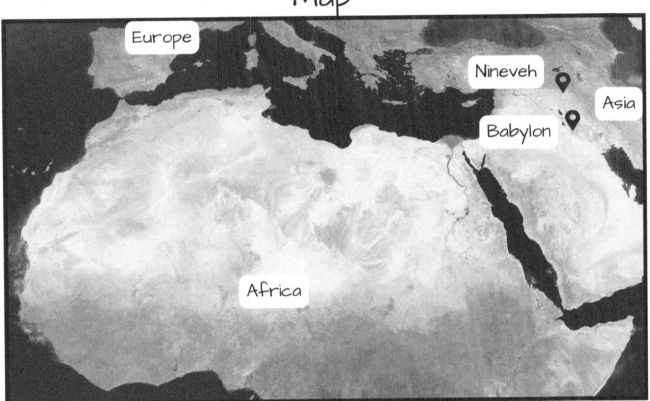

The Hanging Gardens might have been

built in Babylon around 600 B.C.

NAME _____

Hanging Gardens of Babylon

Another theory suggests that King

Sennacherib of Nineveh built the gardens.

The garden's history remains a mystery.

Map of Mediterranean Region

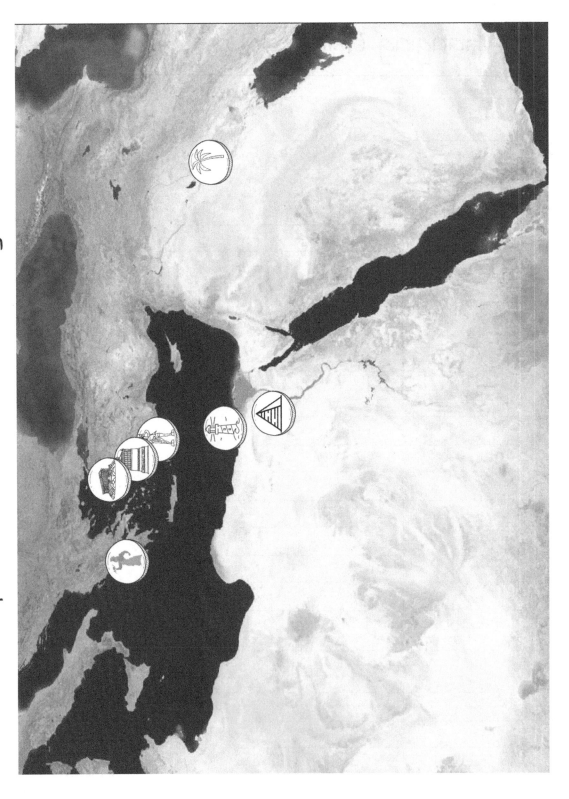

Timeline

approximate dates of construction and destruction
of the Seven Wonders of the Ancient World

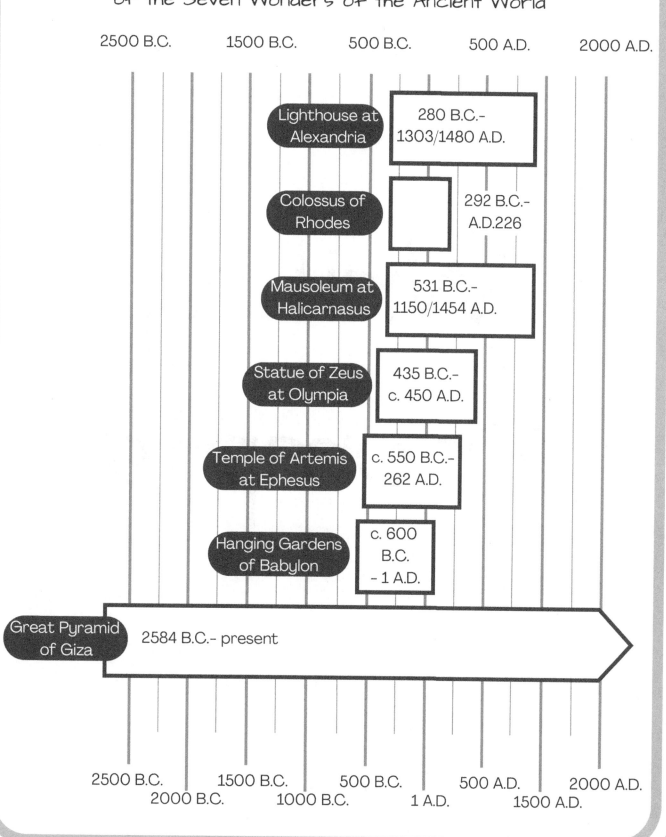

Writing Prompts

NAME _____

Writing Prompt
A Pyramid Builder's Tale

Imagine being a key figure in the construction of the Great Pyramid of Giza. Transport yourself back in time and share your life, experiences, and the incredible journey of building this monumental wonder. Describe the challenges, the innovations, and the daily life of a pyramid builder. What was it like to contribute to this awe-inspiring structure, and what did it take to create one of the world's most iconic monuments? Note: you may find it helpful to read about how the pyramids were built!

_____
_____
_____
_____
_____
_____
_____
_____
_____
_____
_____
_____
_____
_____
_____
_____
_____

Writing Prompt
A Pyramid Builder's Tale

Writing Prompt
A Pyramid Builder's Tale

NAME _____

Writing Prompt
Great Pyramid of Giza

Pretend you visited the Great Pyramid of Giza. Write a postcard from the pyramid to your family, describing your favorite things about the pyramid.

Postcard Front
Decorate the front of the postcard and draw pictures of things you could see while visiting the pyramids (pyramids, camels, etc.). Use colored pencils to color and draw.

Postcard Back
Write a short note to a friend or family member about what you saw.

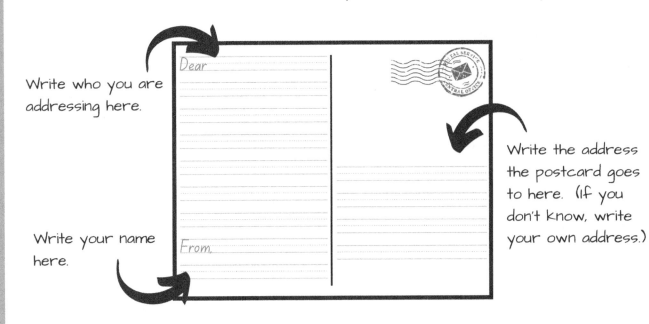

Write who you are addressing here.

Dear

From,

Write your name here.

Write the address the postcard goes to here. (If you don't know, write your own address.)

NAME _____

Postcard front

NAME _____

Postcard back

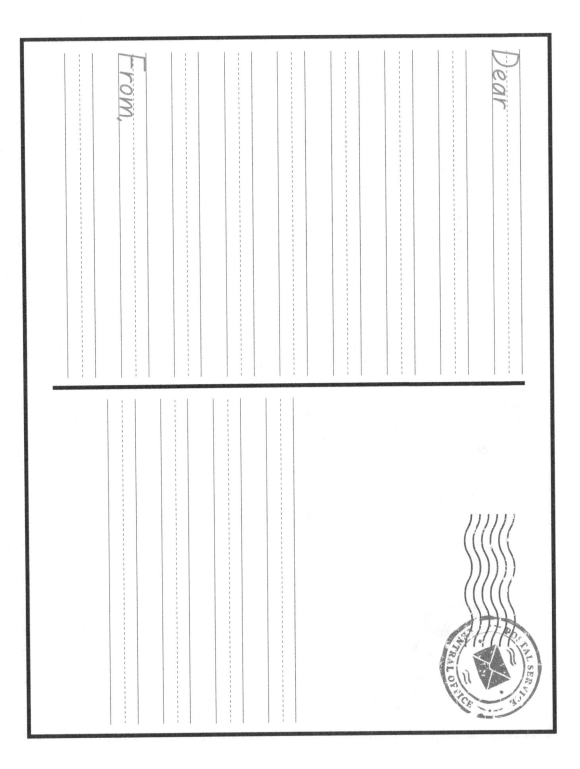

NAME _____

Writing Prompt
Draw Amytis' Dream Garden

Amytis really missed the mountains and green scenery of her homeland, Media. The Hanging Gardens were created to make her feel more at home, with beautiful gardens on different levels that looked just like Media. These gardens had special plants to remind her of the place she loved so much.

Directions: Draw a picture of the Hanging Gardens as you imagine them. Then write a description of your picture.

NAME _____

Writing Prompt
Draw Amytis' Dream Garden

Writing Prompt
The Hanging Gardens

Write a dialogue (a conversation) between King Nebuchadnezzar II and his wife, Amytis, discussing the creation of the Hanging Gardens. You can include information on why he might have created the gardens, description of what it might have looked like, how the plants were watered, and etc.

_____
_____
_____
_____
_____
_____
_____
_____
_____
_____
_____
_____
_____
_____
_____
_____

NAME _____

Writing Prompt
The Hanging Gardens

NAME _____

Writing Prompt
The Statue of Zeus

Look at the scene below. What might be happening? Who are the people in the picture? Write what these people are saying

NAME _____

Writing Prompt
The Statue of Zeus

The city of Olympia in Greece was the location of the Statue of Zeus and where the famous ancient Olympic Games were held. Anyone traveling to the games would have seen the statue.

Write a story from the perspective of an athlete who competed in these games and witnessed the Statue of Zeus. Describe his/her experience.

NAME _____

Writing Prompt
The Statue of Zeus

Writing Prompt
Artemis

Artemis was the Greek goddess of wild animals, the hunt, and vegetation. Look at the picture of Artemis. Then write a description of her.

NAME _____

Writing Prompt
The Greek Times: Breaking News!

Imagine you are a journalist in ancient Greece, reporting on the destruction of the Temple of Artemis in Ephesus.

Write a short article or story discussing what happened. Remember the 5 W's and 1 H as you write (who, what when, where, why, and how).

The following questions can help you write your story:
- What happened to the temple?
- How was the temple destroyed?
- When did it happen?
- How did the people feel? What did they do? Will they rebuild it?
- Where did it happen?

Remember to create a catchy title.

You can write your article on the following page.

THE GREEK TIMES

BREAKING NEWS!

Write your title

Draw a picture of what happened

NAME _____

BREAKING NEWS CONTINUED...

Writing Prompt
Mausoleum Masterpiece

In the Mausoleum, there were numerous thrilling battle scenes. Some of these battles were mythical conflicts, like the ones showing centaurs, lapiths, and Greeks in combat.

Pretend you are an artist chosen to create a bas-relief for the Mausoleum. Your task is to draw a picture and then describe it in words. Imagine and illustrate a captivating scene that you believe would be a perfect addition to the Mausoleum's artwork. Then describe your illustration.

NAME _____

Writing Prompt
Mausoleum Masterpiece

NAME _____

Writing Prompt
The Mausoleum at Halicarnassus

The Mausoleum was elaborately decorated with hundreds of statues, bas-reliefs depicting exciting battles, and a giant marble sculpture of a chariot and horses.

The most talented artists were hired to work on the Mausoleum, including the sculptor, Scopas. Scopas had also overseen the work done on the Temple of Artemis!

If you could interview Scopas, what questions would you ask him? Write these questions. Then imagine what his response might be and write his answer to them.

_____
_____
_____
_____
_____
_____
_____
_____
_____
_____
_____

Writing Prompt
The Mausoleum at Halicarnassus

Writing Prompt
Colossus of Rhodes

Imagine you're a modern engineer tasked with designing a new Colossus for a coastal city. Describe your statue and who would be the inspiration for your statue. You may also draw a picture of your statue.

Writing Prompt
Colossus of Rhodes

NAME _____

Writing Prompt
The Colossus

Finish writing the story. The first few sentences have been written for you.

"As the sun dipped below the horizon, casting a golden hue on the shimmering sea, a young boy stood in the fading light, gazing up at the colossal statue in front of him. Suddenly, a coarse hand landed on his shoulder, and a gruff voice asked, "What brings you here?"

Writing Prompt
The Colossus

NAME _____

Writing Prompt
The Lighthouse

Craft a brief comic detailing a sailor's thrilling journey to Alexandria and his encounter with the renowned Lighthouse of Alexandria. What kind of adventure unfolds during his voyage? Does the sailor face adversaries from foreign lands, sudden tempests, or tumultuous waves in the dead of night? Is the lighthouse a comforting beacon amid chaos or a source of awe and wonder?

NAME _____

Writing Prompt
The Lighthouse of Alexandria

Ruins of the Lighthouse of Alexandria have been discovered on the sea floor near Alexandria, Egypt.   Egypt has considered turning the site into an underwater museum. Create a travel brochure encouraging tourists to visit the underwater museum.

Include the following:

Cover Page
- Title
- Draw or insert a picture
- Write one sentence that encourages people to visit the historical location.

Frequently Asked Questions
- Write three historically accurate questions and answers about the statue or location.

Flip the page

NAME _____

Writing Prompt
The Lighthouse of Alexandria

Reasons to Visit
- State three reasons why tourists should visit the underwater museum.

Facts
- Include three historically accurate facts about the location/statue.

Map & Geography
- Draw (or insert) a map of the historical location with a corresponding list and description of three cities, regions, or landmarks.

Picture
- Additional drawing or picture related to the lighthouse or location.

Frequently Asked Questions

Question _____

Answer _____

Question _____

Answer _____

Question _____

Answer _____

Reasons to Visit

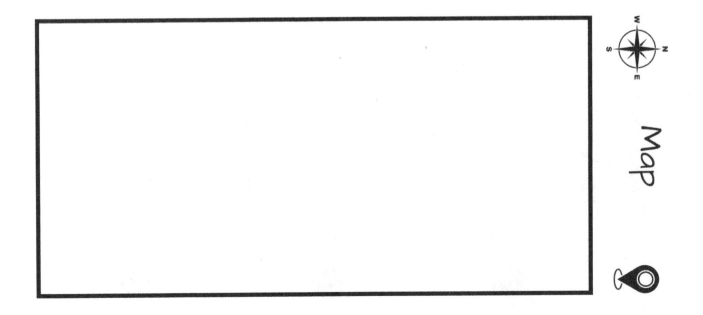

Map

Thank you so much for buying this handwriting practice book!!

I am a small independent publisher and I greatly appreciate your support! A lot of thought and care is put into designing fun and useful publications. Please leave a review so I can continue to create and share great high quality content with everyone and so I know how I am doing!

The following QR code will take you to the Saguaro Bloom Academics Author Page.

SAGUARO BLOOM
ACADEMICS

If you liked this book, here are some other books you may enjoy.

Other Works by Saguaro Bloom Academics

Beginning Cursive: Letters & Letter Connections

This innovative beginning cursive handwriting book is a highly effective program for teaching young children cursive handwriting. This book includes cursive practice, fun activities that help develop skills for fine motor development, and teacher/parent resources

ASIN: B0BPB47BZF

Level 1 Cursive: Words & Sentences

This is a fun interactive handwriting book for children who have learned letters and are ready to write words. This book progresses to short sentences and encourages more independent writing. (Coming Soon)

Level 2 Print & Cursive: Sentences

Fruit of the Spirit- Practice writing sentences of varying lengths with this Christian Bible verse copywork book about the "fruit of the Spirit."

Cornell Notes Notebooks

Cornell notes notebooks are one of the best note taking methods for effective learning. The Kids Cornell Notes Notebooks are specially adapted for elementary students and reluctant writers. Plus, I also offer a wide variety of Cornell Notes Notebooks for teens and adults.

ASIN: B09HFV3Y2Y

ASIN: B09HFV3Y2Y

Book Samples

Beginning Traditional Cursive Handwriting Workbook for Kids
(Grades K-2)

ASIN: B0BPB47BZF

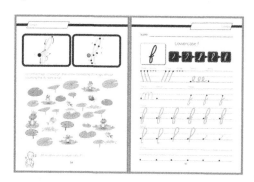

Fun Cursive Handwriting Practice Workbook: Words & Sentences
(Grades K-2)

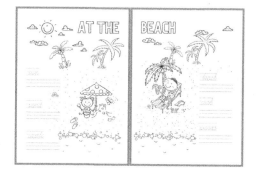

Made in the USA
Las Vegas, NV
14 November 2024

11803298R00052